CW00542621

Animate
Rhys
Campbell

Animate
Copyright © 2023 Rhys Campbell
DARK THIRTY POETRY PUBLISHING
ISBN: 978-1-7397975-8-4

All Rights Reserved

Rhys Campbell
First edition

Artwork by Elijah Bean
Illustrated by Elijah Bean

DTPP7

All rights are reserved. No part of this publication may
be reproduced, stored in a retrieval system or
transmitted in any form or by any means, electronic,
mechanical, photocopying, recording or otherwise,
without prior permission from the author.

DARK
THIRTY
POETRY
PUBLISHING

Dedicated to Johanna Jones

I wish to thank multiple publishers and editors for permission to republish some of the poems.

Poems from Depression is What Killed The Dinosaurs, **Sunday Mornings at the River.**

Pastel Serenity Zine Issue 7
3 Amigos Ink and Splatter Volume 1: Issue 3, **I Ain't Your Marionette.**

Observations

An Ode To Family

They say you can choose your friends,
But you can't choose your family,
Beware of hallmark wisdom
Telling you that blood runs thicker than water,
It silences the nuances of our emotion and connection.
On reflection, What are friends,
If not family?

I find myself blissfully happy with my crew,
We've hit hurricanes,
Where calm waters usually ebb,
We fought off pirates
To come out with a more polished vessel.
The missing nails and sails,
Badges of honour.
The missing limbs and minds,
Trophies from a battle won.
No one makes it to the end without scars
We must accept our vulnerability;
It makes us stronger; in the long run
And this life is a marathon,
There will always be a time when we trip and fall.
If there is no one there to catch you,
There is always gravel.

It is vital to know when to sleep with one eye open,
Some of the crew drink too much
The others sleep too little,

We're all on different levels of the social hierarchy,
Just like ships,
We're made of connected integral parts
Some of us more capable of weathering the storms
And keeping warm
When the bitter winds start to blow.

On the grey days,
We find our tears on each other's shoulders,
When the sun breaks through the clouds,
We can laugh so deeply
Our ribs start to protest
And a different kind of tear manifests,
One that affirms our love unconditional.

Fade

They say as you grow
Things you thought you needed
Will prove you otherwise.
They slip from under the veil of necessity
And fall away in a cascade
No matter how tight your grip.

As tethers tear
You'll realise,
None of them were a power source.
Retinas show you the light,
Serotonin keeps you content.
It all starts with you.
The only true defeat you'll ever know
Is when your mortal coil delivers the final blow.

Make peace with the fact
That your agony means
You're still intact.
You can start anew,
Collecting temporary effects,
Entertaining promises of perpetuity.
Your TV may come with a 10-year warranty
But change is the only guarantee.

The details of faces once adored will fade,
What gave you purpose may lie battered,
Discarded and useless,

And perfect moments
Become perforated with bitterness.
Look for the torment-you'll easily find it,
It never dissipates,
Absences always resonate.
Like a car crash,
You might find that you just can't look away.
Like a masochist,
You can't tune out from the voices telling you
That nothing stayed
Because you made them leave this way.

Time is a construct,
Not a healer.
Sickness stems and is cured in the mind.
We're just animals acting on instinct but it
Doesn't have to be a dog eat dog world.
We can take our failures
And losses and see an
Opportunity for growth,
Instead of reprisal.

We can elevate to new worlds
And realise that
What's in the distance
Doesn't need to be out of mind
Or out of sight.

You get a choice
In what you carry:

Make it light
Or make it heavy
Just leave enough room for love.

Price Tag

I take a step back
To see the people around me
Gloating over what they are taught to admire.

We'd do anything for clout,
Start a bar fight just to win,
Fuck the perfect ten for a tale to tell,
Indebt ourselves for an enviable Instagram story.
Never stopping to question the nature of desire.
Never realising that billboards
Sell greed masquerading as happiness.
Never seeing that our greatest assets are loneliness.

Empty minds fill themselves with excess,
Salivating lips smacking over trends
Keeps the capitalist machine oiled.

Reaching out isn't always easy
But your happiness is your responsibility.
Take hold of those tethers of connection
They'll raise you from the alienation.

Why pay the rent when you can sell your success
On the cost of your personal effects.
Why not take the complimentary anxiety
With each purchase
And wonder how to make ends meet
At the end of the month in cyclical torment?

Living comfortably has no aesthetic,
But it will free you from
The living for the weekend rhetoric.
You can't defy the laws of physics
What goes up
Must come down.
How low can you afford to go?
How many more nights
Do you want to spend with your phone as a dummy
Drinking in global catastrophes,
Polarised hate,
Injustice,
Malpractice,
All of the reasons that tell you
That you're right to hold so much fear
And your creature comforts are justified.

The pressures of this world will get to you,
If you let them.
The hate in this world will devour you,
If you let it.
No man is an island
We need the community to thrive
And love to heal.
Cut through the static.
Climb out of the tunnel vision
That doesn't reflect reality.

Your frustration is universal,

Anyone will tell you,
You just need to listen
You're only as alone as you want to be.

Reaching out isn't always easy
But your happiness is your responsibility.
Take hold of those tethers of connection
They'll raise you from the alienation.

Embers Live On

Continuous surroundings,
An endless landscape of waves.
They've got you like shackled slaves.
You're on lockdown,
It's in your mind.

They've influenced your sight,
A political map,
The belief.
We follow the steps.
I'm giving you insights,
Don't be blind,
Know the meaning of kind.

Breathe what compels you.

The Empire Will Fall

One day,
I hope that I can look to any stranger
And know that they share the same liberty.

One day,
I hope that we'll look back on today
And feel the revelry
Over the time we came together
In our different factions
And collectively demanded action.
No one has the right to stand tall
Using bent backs to enjoy their vantage point.

We'll make no bones
About tearing supremacists from their pedestals.
We'll feel no regret for smashing icons of tyranny.
We'll feel no guilt for tearing apart
Our society which repression built.
We'll make no apology for disrupting
The complacency of systematic oppression.

We'll never lament over silencing the police state
which breeds hateful soldiers
Who foam at the mouth
At the thought of flesh under their heel.
It's time to heal.
We're a global population of similarities.
We all have a story,

Even though they all unfold differently,
Some are scribed in languages we can't read,
And some of the scenes happen
In places we've never been.
Everyone is just trying to finish their chapters
And move onto the next
With the same anticipation, fear, love, and uncertainty
Which flows through us universally.

The vibration of our shared consciousness is elevating,
The despair is losing its grip
And allowing us to extend our hand
And raise the people around us.
It's time to stop fearing dystopias.
Tear up the blueprints and start constructing utopias
in their place.
We'll show the world
This generation's capacity for compassion
Regardless of colour, class and creed.

Those who disagree with us
Will brand us crass and callous,
Look past the cognitive dissonant red mist.
Honour the multitude.
Trigger irreversible change.

With love,
Introduce a new attitude infused with empathy.
We may never fully understand everyone's pain,
But their words will teach you all you need to know

To share their sorrow and allow you solemnly vow
That you'll never stand idly by
And allow them to share the same pain again.

This Isn't Eden

Set your expectation,
Ground it in reality.
Get acquainted with the putridity of decay
And stagnation.
Experience nature in its most elemental form.
The cruelty which manifests
From its malevolence
As it strips existence
From our mortal coil.

Then take a breath.
You're still here without a compass
But the expanses of existence
Will never be road-mapped,
The form of desire can never be defined.
It's malleable to your touch.

Find pleasure in the profound,
The profane,
The perturbed
However it appears.
It's yours to hold,
Impossible to take.
Tempting to relinquish
In the wake of sufferance.

You may feel shadows of others
Encroaching in on your light,

But light is infinite,
Uncommodified.
Trust the extended hands
Outstretched in benevolence,
Separate agendas from the difference.
We're all assimilating
Our ideas of perfection,
Facades take all forms
But we're all in the middle
Basking between light and dark.

Where others lie on the binary
Is not for you to decide.
Throw away the addiction to absolutes,
It's all relative.
Those who take can also give.
The exchange you see
Doesn't define the essence of man.

Our sentience doesn't have to be
Subjugated by whips of fear.
Each crack a new hysteria.

Floor 13

We build zoos,
So we're not the only caged animals.
We chain man's best friend to our wrists
so they don't run away
To see if the concrete is greyer on the other side
Of our worn-down towns
Where women at night
Grip their keys in their fists tight
Where children can't play outside
Because it is too dangerous for their innocence
Where litter has become a part of the landscape
Scattered amongst the homeless
Who ask for change
Only to get a few coins
Thrown into the coffee cup
They found on the floor,
They can't afford it,
Neither can the environment
But society will pay that debt another day.

We push ourselves away from nature
In the name of progress,
But we can't see the stars for the streetlights
We can't breathe the air for the smog
We can't see the sunlight for the high rises
That tower over us,
Their steel, concrete and glass
Separating us from the earth

That we are supposed to feel under our feet,
But step outside this high rise
with bare feet
And you'll be caught by the glass
From bottles thrown
Because people get pleasure
From seeing things break
But I'm a creator,
A lover of nature.

I see everything in this world as intertwined,
Not this artificial reality that screens put in front of me
Where vegan food sparks social media outrage
But in the ecosystem,
We exist in the fine balance of the world
That keeps everything on it sustained
Until we tip the scales enough
That everything that we took for granted
Disappears from in front of us.

If animals had a democratic vote,
We'd be living Animal Farm instead of 1984.
They wouldn't affix themselves to a feudal point
On the left and right binary.
They'd vote to bring humans back in line with
Ecological harmony.

Until nature has its way,
Speak for it.

Soliloquy

Men are taught to suppress emotions
From a young age.
Then when it comes to relationships,
We are expected to express the suppressed.

So maybe it is time to talk about toxic masculinity;
A term bound around so much it loses meaning.

All emotion finds a way out eventually,
Maybe it festers within us first,
Rots us to the core, given the chance.

Recently, I find myself more attracted
To apathy than people.
When things start to feel too real, I choke on the irony,
Of needing to be open and without emotion,
And I'm not the only one reaching
For the arms of a lover,
Only to cower away in the solitude
I attempted to escape when I greet them.

Not all matches spark
Especially with our tendency
To stick with the trauma we know.

Our self-sacrificing bids for independence
Triumph our need to be needed.

I used to pity
The old men walking down the street
Into empty homes where their only friend is the TV,
But the closer I look, I'm looking back at me.

Calling Time

She's not afraid of the dark,
Only the darkness that descends when the sun sets.
It brings back the memories
Of the lonely nights
That followed painful days
When everything felt like the end of the world.

She has lived through enough personal apocalypses
To know that death doesn't come so easily,
It strikes mercilessly
Evading those who beg for it to come.

The innocence of youth
Was taken from her
When trauma sculpted her place in the world.
Her sugar-coated view
Was soured by the bitter breath of her drunk father;
The kisses he'd plant
Once in a blue moon were as stale as his odour
That always choked her
As she held back the tears
That her mum would never see anyway
Her blind eye conveniently fell on the abuse
That would eventually become history
But it was always the same story,
Just with different faces.

No one gets to walk through life unscarred
But some people have enough crosses to bear.
It would break the backs of most,
Yet they still hold their heads high,
They hide the emptiness,
And learn to live under cloak and dagger
To avoid those pitying stares.

In reality,
You'll never know who is close to breaking
You'll never know
When things are cutting too close to the bone.
For her,
There was never any hiding from the lacerations
That seemed to seek out marrow;
Even in a crowded room
Her mind was a clamouring riot,
Synapses firing in all directions
But none of it seemed to be friendly fire.
The warfare exhausted her,
Her cheek never seemed far from the pillow
As the weeks passed and she withered.

The happy pills still left her scratching for serotonin
As she went about her days
That never left her fulfilled,
She'd dread the red letters
Being pushed through the door
She'd dread her kids reaching for sweets
In the supermarket.

Her kids had to learn a thing or two about sacrifice
Yet their bonds grew stronger,
As the wounds on her wrist got deeper
Until they told her
That she had to think bigger
Than just scratching at the surface
Of her skin with metal
To feel something within her control.

One day,
The light switched on behind her eyes
As she realised,
Depression isn't a nemesis
It is a companion,
A memento of past pain
Reminding you of how strong you are
To put one foot in front of the other
When you never wanted
To pick yourself up off the floor.

Her scars became reminders
That she deserved pleasure
More than pain,
Looking at her past showed her
That it didn't have to repeat.

She could resent her past
But that would mean resenting

The strength that she has become.
She could carry the pity,
Knowing that if she didn't help herself,
No one would,
But in the end,
It doesn't matter what you've been through,
You're walking into your future,
Not backwards into your past;
There is a reason why tomorrow isn't called yesterday.

You don't need your abuser's compassion and
permission
To be happy,
You'll never get it from them,
You need to give it to yourself.
Time will only heal,
If you let it.

Penance

Through The Threads Of Reality

I am grateful for the day, mostly.
But sometimes,
A discontented haze glazes appreciation for life,
For the clockwork hum of functioning anatomy,
Or the birds singing chorally
And allowing us to enjoy their melodies.

Some days, it's easy to forget.
It's easy to drown out the sound,
Let something else consume us instead,
Leave blinkers on red
Before apathetically resigning to our pillow
And whispering to it our melancholy.

Some carry their past as a dead weight,
Making it harder for them to cross the finish line
For the races, we start and finish every day.
I harness mine as protection,
A key to the future
Where all that matters is the present.

Every day is a journey,
So I pack my bags ready for what happens next.
I make my travel guide
By formulating the ways
I can purge my mind
Of the burdens which relentlessly scratch away
At the base of my skull.

I still hear the echoes of idyllic idioms
Which are never grounded in reality.
"Time will tell..."
"Time is the greatest healer..."

Imagine,
If we were taught what freedom tastes like.
Imagine,
The sticky-sweet nectar of mental liberation
Being dripped onto your tongue,
Allowing you to savour how it feels to be free
From insecurity,
Anxiety,
And panic attacks which rip the ground
From Beneath our feet,
Draw sensation from our lips,
Make our rhythmic pulses feel like lacerating stings.
My afflictions aren't my enemies.
I wear them with no hostility,
Knowing I can take them off
With wishful thinking,
And relinquishing the sinking feelings
Which pull me down when I entertain the idea
That I need to be punished for being human.

There were days when I was afraid of the sun
And the rays which illuminate everything
I didn't want to see,
There were days when the only safe place was

The space in my dreams,
Where I could run free and explore
New realities under my orchestration.

Now, I embrace any effervescence
The sky throws my way,
I pull it towards me and live fully
With my open eyes
And open mind
Opening up new possibilities,
Every day is a new premiere
And everyone has an invitation to the theatre.
The ticket is my smile,
The price is peace.

I seek to spread addiction to being inspired,
Instead of what will make you numb and wired.
My work started with me,
But it will end by showing the world we're all one.
If you take my view,
You'll see what I see
And it's so beautiful to see
The delicacy of our temporary existence,
And our impermanent nature
Laced with humility and compassion.

My work is for unity, one destiny. All in harmony.
Peace has been there all along,
Hiding in the shadow of materialism and conformity.
Social constructions attempted to mould us,

But let's shatter them to dust
With the pride in our uniqueness,
And understanding of the purity
In individual presence.

Let your dreams carry you,
Be whatever awakens you.

Desolated

Under the knife of pain,
Help me out of these chains,
Chains caused by misery.

I always wanted you to stay.
I thought I was lost,
You pulled me ceaselessly.
On this desolate bed, I lay.
All I sense is trouble,
Conceived by familiar problems.

Drag me closer,
Pluck away every part of me,
As I feel I'm closer,
I can no longer see.

End this suffering,
I'm still aching,
I'm living and feeling.
Always searching
And connecting with souls,
I have lost these feelings of old.

People are torn,
From which they will grow.
Every problem is not a part of you.
This is not a contention,
I shouldn't have to mention this,

Let go of it all.

Plural Destinations

This ticking time bomb
Of our very existence perplexed me.
How life and death co-exist,
Spectating a collection of moments.
Sometimes I need a reminder that life
Is an experience, not an observation.
Sometimes I don't feel good,
Sometimes I get stuck in that downward spiral,
Falling into that place.
That place that feels so deep you can't climb out,
A mental prison of sorrow.
Which can make it so hard to see tomorrow
Because in my head I've already died.
Yet there's a flesh prison still here navigating the
Experience of life.

We're all experiencing the same hallucination,
Working every day tirelessly
Trying to find our place in this world.
What am I supposed to do as a career?
What works for me to afford a house in the generation
Of underachievers who can't afford a train ticket
Or juice with nutritional value?
We take every day for granted.
Wasting time by consuming materialistic propaganda,
Binge-watching Netflix shows until our eyes dry out
After selecting 'continue watching' at least six times.

Instead, we could've been investing our time in
Colonising mars, buying up PayPal or producing
Electric sports cars.
How do we know our destiny?
The one depicted for us is the stars.
Is it written in the palms of our hands, tarot cards or
told to us in dreams?
How did Musk discover his passions?
What led him down the path
Of a relentless work ethic?
I guess his answer would be simple,
He loved the idea and he did it, He made it happen.

Am I destined to be a writer?
Or am I destined to distribute boxes
Or become a plumber and clean out dirty pipes?
Am I expected to settle with a lover I feel no spark
with or a lover
That treats me like dirt but at least I feel something?
Will I ever find what I'm looking for?

Maybe I'll be happy with no money
As long as I have the perfect someone,
Or will I be happy with the perfect job
And perfect house still searching to fill the void?

Elysian Gates

When was the last time you opened your eyes?
Prise them wide,
The world is waiting for you
While you're absorbed by tyrannical matter.
A trembling sheep,
Bleating without character.
Confront your autonomous mind,
Harness the power inside,
Connect the dots,
Take the thread between your fingers
And weave your fabric of existence.

There should be no doors to your mind,
Locking out understanding of human experience
In all of its perplexing variance.

Join me,
As I close my eyes and pull up the scars,
Viewing from afar.
As I harness my knowledge of how to repair,
Taught to me by despair.
Distance doesn't heal,
Only disguises.
Through desperation
We cloak ourselves with camouflage.
But take a look underneath,
Gaze into the constellations
Of stubborn stars

Mapping out your journey,
You may already see
That you're half-way there.
Push further,
Find the strength you stowed in unsealed boxes.
It's always been right there to find
And realise your capacity for regeneration,
Once you free yourself from the emancipation
Of trying to build something so strong
On weak foundations.

Go deep underground,
Dig out the safety and love
Which always lay amongst the dirt and tar
And exhume peace.

We all carry secrets
Never to be spoken.
But what is the past to the future;
Nothing but a memory.
If we don't make shame the essence of who we are-
Even if you're in the gutter-
Grab a foothold
And stand your ground.
The ladder rungs will manifest
Once you've got the strength to climb.
Your hands will never be free
If you cling to the bottle.
Sobriety strips the numb comfort
Which makes it so easy to keep our eyes shut

From the world.
Keep them open,
See the possibility that life isn't what it seems.
Be the positive change in a progressive world,
Make enough ripples in the water
That they'd create a tsunami collectively:
Be the person you aspire to be.

It doesn't matter
How deep you have to dig into yourself to heal,
If you can't find a way to live life with love.
Love is the only thing that matters,
Love one another.
We are one.

Knight Lacking Silver Armour

You were a rose with hidden thorns
That I foolishly came to touch,
I have to stop, thoughts of scorn
There's no diamond in the rough.

You gave birth to crooked fears
Never thought, love holds such grim tears.
I'm tired of swollen eyes and broken hearts
Why draw blood on damn old scars?

I'm left wondering to myself...

What if I don't make you happy?
What if I'm not enough?
And suddenly you confirmed...

I was almost, and almost was never enough.
You left 'cause I wasn't a prince,
Just a knight lacking silver armour.
You never wanted me, you were never happy
Because all of that is found in him.

Crimson lips held poison in her tongue,
A love not as perfect as the tales.
Tempted from the ceiling to be hung
'Cause love was never meant to sail.

Like the darkness of my room

I quivered at my chilly gloom
Like the sadness in my smile
I sobbed without a pleasant style.

Ashes

Under your dark cascading blanket,
I closed my eyes and such.
A tender swift caress
From the evening summer hush.

I savoured your very lips
From the black of air you breathe.
I lusted for the crisps
That I tasted from your teeth.

Addicted to your charm,
I was in for a swirling hell
From the demons that caused harm
To the skins of my shell.

I lived for the beating lie,
The very poisons of my life.
Oh, man.
I feel like I'm gonna die,
And I'm in for a lot of strife.

It had been centuries since then,
When love had paved its way
From the clock of greatest sins;
It ripped me, failing you to stay.

I always knew that good things come to an end,
Like how the flowers close in snow

These wound would not so gracefully mend,
I knew it when you watched the blood flow.

My heart bled while you stood to stare
And new seasons blew my silver hair.
Yesterday's gloom chains my soul
On my chest, betrayal drilled a hole.

I thought tricks were only done by clowns,
They never tend to lie.
As I walked in empty halls
All I see are greyish skies.

I cannot believe as I carried you,
In my lonely, seeking arms
You were painting other hues
In our canvas, blue and black.

Severed by fissures from the earth
I fixed the mess you made,
Learned from a woman since my birth
That love was always something meant to stay.

Love was meant to fill you to the brim,
To help you grow and rise.

About You

Endless thoughts
And a clock going tick tock.
Countless nights,
I've felt your bite.

One day,
I'll remember why
I always pushed you
From my thoughts.

Taking a step back
To admire peaceful endings,
Why can't you?
Let me bite that apple,
Embrace your sin,
Your thoughts
So sickening,
Eve give me more.

Distant paths
Somehow meet
A precious rose
With fierce thorns.
We hurt,
We suffer,
We have to find ourselves.

Explain this,

You owe me that.
Give me a reason
To believe the lies you spat.

Trials

These tedious trials
I have created for myself.
Through the fierce storms,
A battle in my head,
A battle for one thing;
A battle for composure.
My only victory entails
Bettering the life I'm living,
I am already experiencing paradise,
Paradise is my day to day life.
To be one step ahead
Without action is nothing.

What I want is to be one step
Ahead to ease this creation,
To ease the life of others,
So we love one another.

What does it mean to be honest?
What does it mean to be humble?
What does it mean to be without trouble?
That's not found buried at the bottom of a bottle.
Are you questioning things?
That's the first step; to make a change.
This isn't single-player game,
This is a multiplayer game.
The first step is to look at yourself
And remember you're not like anyone else.

Not trying to be like others,
No need to fit in with your brothers.

Now ask yourself
Will you make it better?
Make your existence a better place to be
A better way to see
You are glory;
You are stardust experiencing the human condition.
We are the paint on a canvas
Ascending and searching galaxies.

We're all searching for something to create a legacy.
Yet I can only blossom if I am doing the things I desire.
The things I love.
I will never fall victim to the shadows
That creep into selfish desires.
Into the unknown, I venture.

This life is about taking risks.
Choosing what might break you,
will be what makes you.

I was swimming with loads of leeches,
Now I'm swimming on the beaches.
Sick of those that were trialling me.
This is far from conformity,
I just know the angels are waiting to greet me.

I've made mistakes,

I will continue to pay,
Please forgive me.

You're never going to be perfect in the eyes of another,
The love you show the world
Will earn respect from others.
Praying for the world to come together.
We're all blinded by temporary satisfactions,
Always working too fast
To pull away from the action.
You can follow my advice,
But believe me, there are contradictions.
For it is the mistakes
I have made that allowed me to grow.

When I Met Poetry (Men Don't Feel)

Before my mind was fully formed,
Books never interested me.
What did it matter if there were new worlds inside?
Fiction didn't capture my imagination,
It didn't match mine either.

One day, on my countless shelves
I noticed poetry hiding behind a plain cover.
There wasn't a story to tell
Just a new way to see the world I already knew,
I thumbed the pages,
Finding new ways to understand
The numbness in pain,
The chaos of chance,
The experiences which would tell me
Never to feel the same
Until the resonance felt like salt in the wound.

When relatable content felt like torment
My lexicon became limp,
I started to evade my triggers
I forgot what it was like to feel
Before I hit rock bottom,
And exhumed my passion for expression.

Today,

I'm full of feeling
Ready to share my story,
Of endless nights
Between the sheets with anxiety
With so much weight in my head,
I couldn't lift it from the pillow.

I wondered what happy childhood nostalgia felt like,
All I had was memories
Of when I was young and silent,
Unable to stutter words
That would allude to my insecurities
Which stemmed from inside
But when it came to placing blame,
My reflection would hide.

I kept the door to humble hearts locked
Through fear of being chewed through
And never being whole enough to find someone new.
The unconfounded anxiety twisted my words
Ensuring what I meant never came through
They were just sound vibrations with no resonation.

I forgot what it meant to feel with words.
I could only deal
With uncertainty and absurdity
When nights would roll around,
I'd toss,
Turn
And keep the dangers

Of this world on repeat.

Why is there free speech
If I'm shut down every time I speak?

Anxiety is my closest friend, why won't it let me sleep?

This is panic attack number six this week.
I was withered,
Shaken and weak
From the negativity,
I'd soak up
Before it dampened my sheets in sweat.

What made you a part of me, anxiety?

Can't you set me free?

I still fear giving a spare key to my heart,
But I'm getting there
Maybe I'm ready enough to find another toothbrush
Next to mine from time to time.

There are so many things I would have vocalised
If only I wasn't so terrified
In the days before comfort crept in and bathed me
In a warm desire to be listened to without fear.

From that day,
My love for words rose higher

Than any wave of anxiety.

For a lifetime,
It felt I had nothing to lose
But now I can see
The true nature of reality;
My former perception was pulled from the grave
I dug myself into.

I spent entire nights
Marching in the trenches of my bed
After days slept away.

Anxiety has never been fond of me
But the cruellest teachers
Are the best ones you'll ever have.

Reflections

A Lesson In Colour

I'm a mouthpiece,
Spitting ways to stay sane,
But I can't remember the last time
My Mind knew peace from pain.

I turn to philosophy for reason,
Only to find my nihilism more justified.
I'm riding burning tides
Revisiting all the times I've lied
And become the villain
Instead of the protagonist.
After turning plot twists into holes.
I'll never be a best-seller;
Just the guy that messed around
With the rules of music,
Attempting to portray
A narrative of the unmaterialistic.

Embracing optimism
Means leaving realism behind
Because I want to be optimistic,
I want to be this and that
Quenching the desperate thirst
To placate and enlighten the masses.
Maybe all it will take
Is one more epiphany
To bring back meaning.

I want to wrap the world in poetry
But I'm just trying to say
That I want to be free,
Free of judgement,
Lacking in ego,
Apologetic,
Apathetic to accolades,
You'll see it if you read
Between the lines
Of my neurology and linguistics.

Truthfully,
Most of the time I'm unenthusiastic
Sapped dry by
Acceptance of failure.
Bruised by hitting rock-bottom
Too many times,
Refusing to get up
From my self-induced low points.
I'm always just one contortion
Away from disjointing,
Counting on creativity
To act as a suture
And hold me together
For long enough
For me to breathe,
Forget about the ego,
And look at the world with colour.

Here lies a lesson in expression.

Hostility

I am being,
Sitting with life,
Nothing defined or known.

Everything is as it is,
I now have my place,
I am content
With what I have.

But happiness isn't defined
By situation,
I will forever wander
In the unknown.

Whilst knowing
I don't need
To play any role,
Everything is as it is.

The Learning Curve

Don't be the outlier who challenges archetypes,
Who see stereotypes as trite.
Squeeze your personality into this mould,
Don't fall outside of the lines,
That's what we are told
Before we are old enough to know
That there is more than one way to grow.

It isn't the children failing in the education system.
It's the system failing the children,
The ones who communicate best through music
The ones without art would lose it
The ones who already know
They're not an aspiring mathematician.
Teachers are so quick to show us
The different types of angles
But never share different points of view,
They keep it secret
That no one can excel in everything,
Failing grades cascade around confusion
Chipping away at confidence
Each failed exam, the threat of negative consequence.

How different would society be
If education was made fair,
Perhaps more people
Would be able to hear their calling,
Maybe it would be easy to see

That the educational system
Is as flawed as the corrupt economic system
And industrial-military complex.

With every year that passes
I count the missed opportunities for real education.
Why didn't you tell me
That I'd have to invest in emotional intelligence?
Why didn't you teach me that people out there
Will use my mind against me?
Why did you leave me to ponder the meaning of life
When the simple answer is,
"Whatever you want it to be".

Kids are taught about the old world,
Not the world they have to navigate.
Prepare them for the complex system
Of finance, taxes and law.
Empower them by introducing them to true nutrition,
Not just spinning the facts that line the pockets of
pharmaceutical companies.
Our lifestyle is killing us.
Each meal can lead us closer to a disease
That can bankrupt us.

Mindfulness may never be mandatory
In the curriculum,
But you can introduce it to the rhythm of life.
You can facilitate generations growing together happy,
Avoiding mental health labels

That will follow kids to the grave,
Just one act of kindness
Can stand in the way of suicide,
You'll probably never know which
But you can be content,
Knowing that you helped the world
To keep on growing.

You don't have to be perfect for kids to look up to you.
Show them the inevitability of imperfection.
Show them the beauty in flaws.
Show them they haven't been cast into a new system
Aged eighteen all alone.

The Construction Of Fear

What if the news turned its gaze away
From the atrocities,
And focused on the acts of kindness
That make this world worth living in.

What if the media gave us good examples to follow
Instead of giving us more justification for nihilism.

What if everyone had a thirst for emotional knowledge
Instead of the need for gossip on savages.

We all have that one friend
That watches the news every day
And carries the fear into their lives,
In their day to day tasks,
On their day to day drives.

They say chaos is order,
Well yes
This is true
But let's introduce something new.

Lost In Translation

Cat got your tongue, kid?
Find a way to sharpen that wit
And stop mumbling.

The voices in my head
Are so much more eloquent than me;
I stutter when I attempt to translate their IQ.

Every time I try to communicate,
Complicated feelings fumble in my throat
Until I start to choke
Then the fear kicks in again
And I can barely speak my own name.

I know I'm not the only one
I know how much of other people's
Intelligence I'm missing out on.

Inanimate

Birds Of Prey

As we drive through,
The crowded streets.
I see men who've worn
Their battlesuits.

Fury cackled
As words were etched
To express demands
From the sea of crowds.

As I delve into
Their pools of brown,
I see caged birds
With clipped wings.

With no escape
They sang a song,
Furious melodies
From their hearts.

They sang against
Deceptive monsters,
Who deprived the birds
Of their freedom.

While I, the free bird,
The bird with wings,
Watched them sing

Their voices filled with pain.

With closed eyes,
My wings flapped
And I sang at once
For one very reason.

They are the birds of prey,
As the free bird,
It would not take long
Before my wings are clipped.

I Thought Stars Were Yellow

Precious starry night,
You've held little dots
Twinkling in your embrace
Of black and blue.

We've laid our blankets
On the sweetest grass,
With summer dews
On our backs.

I tried to turn from
The shadows over the hill,
But the gloomy silhouette
Took me in its arms.

I have seen
The light of tomorrow,
But it's just a lie
Coated in paint of white.

Darkest hollow night,
Stars were supposed to be yellow
But they were just dots
In your lonely dark embrace.

The Monkey Will Bite

Monkey see
Monkeys do.
What do we know
To be true?

Everything is give and take,
But keep it smooth
And don't bite
More than you can chew.

Anthropocene

Everything will subside
If we continue to oversupply
And divide our populations,
Whilst they are denied
Basic human rights
Something which
Should be implied.
This is an obvious
Consequence of
Too much pride.

We paint the ocean red
And when everything is gone,
It will remain unsaid.
They do not know what they do
But we have everything to lose
Because the ocean
Is meant to stay,
If we continue our ways
It'll bite back
And we'll be washed away.

The deep blue sea
Is now painted red
With lifeless sentient beings
Due to a lack of understanding.
A connected consciousness
Subsided because of those misguided.

The breath of the planet is wheezy,
Its blood drained and
Spilt onto another's page.
Let's come together,
Unite and listen to the earth
Overconsumption we must abstain from.

Pluviophile

She loved the rain,
Finding calmness in the noise,
The grey skies bringing poise.

She noticed the turbulent world
Go quiet and everyone
Switch off their mental riots.
The sound of the patters
Acted as white noise
And the intermittent overcast
Allowed the sweetest
Of aromas to deploy.

What may seem gloomy to some
Is a transcendental moment to one.
Her eyes wandered to
The springing drips from leaves
And the rose-coloured clouds,
As she patiently waited
For that sun break
Allowing a rainbow to grow.

Eventually,
It broke into the night
And to her delight
The heavy rain reignites.

Seventh

If you could study vibrations,
It would bring together nations.
This is why my words are to music,
I'm feeling the love I may as well use it.

I will make the change,
Choosing the lane
And flowing within

Refresh those minds giving negativity,
I refuse the influence
Please take it away from me,
Retracting and chewing,
Let go and spew it.

High on a mountain,
I feel the positive flow.
Feeling the radiance
I feel the light glow.
Live in the moment,
I move with the flow,
I'm not politically charged
And I ain't no fraud.

I will make the change,
I'm flowing within.
Not choosing a lane
And within flowing.

Gonna move today,
Not gonna lose today.
To clear the air
On another's breath,
Gonna give the world the best,
Don't taunt me,
I will detest.
Another kingdom of sorrow,
Let's make the change
And not stay the same.

Get up!

Animate

Gaia's Heartbeat

Relinquish control,
Let the rhythm of your breath
Do more than fill your lungs,
Allow it to centre you
As you pull your body out of the sand.

Distance yourself from the bottom feeders.
You know better than to take on their karma;
You get what you put out.
Leave them to look between the lines
In Lucifer's riddles
And collect senseless crosses to bear,
Instead of contributing
To the collective strength of humanity.
Our power is sufficient,
Yet we are helpless.

Let the spotlight of your mind's eye
Drift away from them,
Surrender to yourself instead,
Feel the peace that comes to heart
Accept it without question,
Apprehension is above our pay grade.

Find true form,
Find your platform for transformation
Where you can do what defines you

And the rest will be taken care of.

Our deepest fears stem from separation,
But vulnerability can be beautiful
Because the only definitive truth
Is that the experience of life is individual.

Between your truth and mine,
There's a cumulative space for compromise
And understanding of differentiation;
Our hearts hold the pathways
Woven with invisible material
But it is just as real as the mist
In our clouded minds that are at strife
With our overly occupied world.

Close your eyes.
Take a breath
Feel Gaia flow through you.
This is what the ancients knew,
And now,
So do you.

Hemnes

What is the future
Without growing and learning from our mistakes?
Things are changing,
Time is morphing
And I'm lost in its perplexing nature.

The character of I
Is lost in the labyrinth.
It's like the past,
Present and future are merely words.
Rather than something of meaning,
Because the past is something of the present
And the present holds the future.

We are left to our own devices of free will,
Exploring the journey of life,
That is sempiternal.
We are lacking in instructions
Like the HEMNES dresser from the infamous IKEA.

Some believe there is a formulated way,
Some believe things stay the same
Or it seems like I'm looking for something to blame.

Whilst you're witnessing
This electromagnetic frequency,
Encapsulating my rambles,
Lacking originality,

Because I,
Like everyone,
Have been built on influences.
Nonetheless,
We collect our broken shards
Of glass and glue them together,
In an individual manner.

I know this is part of something bigger than me,
Something that travels,
Through the threads of the universe
And through collective consciousness.
This substance is on the other side of fractals,
Taking on a contrasting connotation to organisational,
Transported via cymatics.

This piece portrays unity,
Projections of the heart,
Empathetic and perceptive,
In a form of art.

Perhaps I need to be self-honouring,
Embody gratitude,
To acknowledge
The universe so divine.

Perhaps I'm just rambling.
Yeah, I'm just rambling.

Divination

Listen to others and understand
There's a world to discover.
Primordial forces run in me deep,
The spiral of life
Flows through what I speak.

Light illuminates flesh
Becoming all to be,
Everything is working
In the best-case scenario.

Uniqueness is in
How we decode reality.
Mystical experiences
Have led me to the truth:
This is, my eternal pursuit.

There is separateness
From I that transitions
To me being conscious,
Affined to selflessness.

Don't let the senses distract,
Do not perceive as
What you lack.
For the soul is eternal
But the body is primaeval.

Humanity is emotionally
Involved with no diversion,
A political excursion,
A transcendental submersion.

You don't need to
Define yourself,
Don't idolise
And penalise,
Don't react in anger,
Don't attack the person.

Indiscriminate unity,
Let's grow as one,
Be as one,
We are one.

There's a world to discover
Out here on the other side.
Concealed from the eyes
Of the thinking mind,
On the edge of sanity,
Through the threads of reality.

I Am That I am

The creative principle
In the sea of wisdom,
The infinite ship of light,
I am that I am.

The glory of the sun
Shines past me.
The glory of the moon
Shines on me.
But I will sail
The ship of light,
The divine spark,
The creative principle.

In the sea of wisdom,
The infinite sea of light.

Progressive in nature,
Eternal and blissful.
Increasing duration
In spiritual existence.
Challenge beliefs,
Break the barriers.
I am that I am.

Unity

I wish to live in gratitude,
Admiration of beauty
Is the optimum mindset.
Why can't we see
There is beauty everywhere?

I watched as plants grew,
To learn the lesson
That everything is
In the flow,
Everything is connected
And everything is one.

There are challenges,
We all lack,
We all fall,
But we are never without.

Let's cut out single-minded
Pursuits of judgement,
Let's catch ourselves
In those downward spirals,
Let's evolve internally and externally.
Don't give the ego warning,
Like a double-blind study,
Let it happen.

Moving Forward | Moving Backwards (Scattered Meditative Thoughts Collected)

We're stuck here,
Left to fend for our own needs.
We turn time searching for what it is we need.
Tagged with names at birth,
Our society is stuck
Moving in circles.
We can hide,
For only so long
Before life catches up.

What will it be?
Our future's generation
Left in devastation,
With deficiency
Of sophistication.
Will it be
An assembly line
Of emotionless beings?
No ambitions,
Only a focus on what
These robots are saying.

The sky is so dark
Due to the greed
In existence

And those that we hold high.
I'll say it again,
We can break into the light.

Speaking like Hanuman
Ram, Ram, Ram.
There are moments
When we open our eyes
To the disruption of the world.
It is the illusion of the time
In which we suffer.
It is the journey in which we move.
We start to split,
With a tick.

Do not move in the motion
That is offset,
Go with the flow,
I promise,
You won't feel low.
Smile, you will feel a glow

Goals and aspirations
What does this mean?
For those are to be,
This is not seen.
It is the law of one.
We are the creators.
Listen to yourself,
Feel the moment.

Clarity exists in the present,
Let go of materialism
And remove the ego.

When I close my eyes,
I show gratitude.
This is prosperity,
It is the law of one.
I do not aspire,
I am my creation.
Desire is not prosperous,
Become what you are.
Imagination exists to create.
Into the unknown, we venture.

How do you achieve victory
If you don't try?
In my dreams,
What is that you
Wish to accomplish?
Do you want to be stuck
In the darkness of night?
You can break into the light.

Breathe

This poem is dedicated to me.
It is my path to a brighter perspective.
Meander down it with me,
Feel each step release you from what you were
As you start to see another way to be.

Welcome to the new earth.
Everyone eats for free,
No one asks you for conformity
Only authenticity without uniform.

This road will teach you
That trying to be normal
Is trying to fit into a mould of perfection
No one has ever been able to achieve.
Fallen icons are just as infallible as the rest of us.
Just look at Bowie and his drug dependency
How is he any different
From the residents of LA's tent city?
He was a star, shining in the spotlight;
In the dark, he wrestled with psychosis.
What hope does the rest of us have in this world of
obscurity and expectation?

Our values are invalid
Societal demands are unwarranted.
Stop denying your true nature
Set fire to the facades,

Find no apology in your expression.
Find the humour in seriousness,
Laugh through the smoke
As constructs crumble around you
And those who don't share your vision scream
Through fear of losing the system
After they've invested in it for so long.

It takes courage
To stay true to the world;
This complex phenomenon
Loosely defined by time and space.
Grace will get you there,
Canter at your own pace.

You can't change the nature
Of humanity single-handedly;
You'll need to accept
The monkey-see-monkey-do mentality,
In this fish eat fish town.
Savages walk amongst us;
You don't need to fall in line with them
Or allow them to consume your time.
Look for the positivity amidst the chaos
In society that influences us to be worthless.
The truth is that we are worthy.
We're all learning lessons,
Moving as meditative regressions,
We're the result of endless timelines ventures.

Find your centre.
Find your place.
Find your worth.
Don't look to pre-existing values
And the insecurities that bleed through
The cracks of our society,
Look to your soul to tell you what you need.
Most of the time,
You'll find that you simply need to breathe.

Waves

We're incorporating linear parallels in lunar tradition,
Locked in linguistic prophecies
Finding ourselves passively on the path
Of least resistance.
It's only the independent world
Breaking through into transcendence.

Finally the dissonant understand,
They can finally hear the call for vulnerability,
The necessity of true form,
Strip back the cold-hard veneer,
Unshackle yourselves from the shadow
Of external narratives.

You are just a carbon copy in everyone else's mind.
Remain in the present chapter,
History repeats
And tomorrow will be today when the sun hits.
We're just bags of flesh and bones
Encased in alpha suits,
Thinking fists first with passivity tattooed
On the bruised knuckles we brandish.

Intuition brings circumstance,
Circumstance brings intuition.
While serpentine tongues
Spit venom
Down the spines,

Transposing under optical luminescence.

There will always be uninvited days
Of languor-littered paralysis
But purpose will manifest,
Once you grasp for it
With the reach of your own desire.

Momentum may be reticent,
But complacency is the thread which causes.
The fabric of our reality to unravel
Revealing dormant trauma
And our need for exhalation.

Our obsession with being on the right path
Blinds us to those collisions which happen every day,
The cutting of lanes,
Ignorance when it's your right of way.
Everyone's out to overtake the learner drivers,
Testing the waters of their velocity.

We're all somewhere in the process
Rushing to go nowhere,
Not behind the wheel
But in our minds.
Imagine if we all moved at the same pace.
Imagine.

Goleuo

My vision crystalline as I open my eyes
At the crack of dawn,
Scratching away at the sleep surrounding my eyelids,
A good indication of a peacefully deep slumber.

My skin shed because today's a new day,
I stretch and manoeuvre out of the sheets.
Today I'm feeling glad,
Today I will what do makes me happy
And today I'm not worrying about the consequences.

It is said,
Do what thou wilt,
But do not do what affects others.
So if that is at the core of our instinctual actions,
Why are we ever swayed from our happiness?

Today I'm helping others,
Today is about community
And today I'm not worrying about anything,
Other than commemorating
And sharing the pleasures of existence.

There will be some who challenge your glow.
Don't you worry about artificial smiles,
Under no obligation do you have to push
False positivity on them
Because bears don't even eat porridge.

Nothing is a straight line,
But a spiral.

The Muse

I write because I need to,
An expressionist needs an outlet
Like a fire needs a spark to glow.

I'm divinely guided by these feelings
That refuse to subside,
Until they spill onto the page
As an incarnation of every emotion
That breezes through these hollow bones.

My words have taught me wrong from right,
They guide me through this discordant society
That makes it almost impossible
To cut through the noise
To find true meaning.
I keep my feelings tight
To take the weight off my chest,
My vocabulary is the duress
That keeps meaningless at bay,
As long as I can spit beauty on the page
Through parables and metaphors
I've got something worth living for.

Gravity

Heavy breaths fall around the basslines
As the music drones with euphoria.

Heart-pounding screams
Kick around the breakdowns,
The aroma of sweat and beer slick in the air,
Hair damp with sweat
But we've never felt so beautiful,
So free,
Right here
This is the true meaning of unity.

We slam into each other
As though gravity demands it
But we'd be fooling ourselves
If we said it was anything
But an impulse of aggression.

Ouroboros

Our potential for compassion and connectivity is
stifled in this vicious cycle of narcissism.

Our biggest fears lie in the slip of facades,
The unveiling of our human nature.
Even our fears can't think bigger than ourselves.
Our obsession with individuality
Created an unstable community;
We've neglected our foundations
While giving ourselves a facelift.

In these precarious times, communal instincts kick in.
If you can look past introspection,
A siren call to the hostility, deterioration
And toxic tribalism will entice you towards integrity.

The best stories are the ones that surface
From the dark,
Be on the right side of the story.

About The Author

Rhys Campbell resides on the small island of Bermuda, a rock hidden away in the Atlantic ocean. Although he was born Bermudian he grew up in Cardiff, Wales which moulded him to be the person he is today. Self-taught, he started writing for himself at the tender age of 14.

Rhys often conveys his poetry within the verbalised art form that is spoken word. You can find his work on all major streaming platforms usually complemented with ambient instrumentals to further ensure the impact of the narratives illustrated.

@rhysc.ampbell

RELEASED BY DARK THIRTY POETRY

Printed in Great Britain
by Amazon

32183597R00059